Lovely Lampshades

Annien Teubes

δελος

CAPE TOWN

A "bare light" is a problem one is often confronted with in the process of brightening a home with creative needlework or interior decorating. On the following pages I present some ideas for solving this problem. By covering a ceiling or table lamp with a beautiful shade, you can work wonders.

Make a pretty lampshade the focal point in a room, or let it form part of the theme of a room.

I am grateful for the inspiration from Him who makes anything possible, and to my family and parents for their support. I also wish to thank Marike and Heleen for their assistance and encouragement, and Elna Slabber for her contribution.

Acknowledgements

DMC for all the sewing thread
Prima Toys for "Dreambaby" doll
Pep Stores, Moorreesburg, for the styling material
Flowers by Estelle for the flowers used for styling

40 Heerengracht, Cape Town

Also available in Afrikaans as *Fleurige Lampskerms*

Photography by André Stander
Typography by Corrine Hoffman
Cover design by Lou and Joy Wrench
Typeset in 10 on 12 pt Optima by Unifoto, Cape Town
Printed and bound by Blackshaws, Cape Town

First edition, first impression 1990

ISBN 1-86826-131-X

Contents

Introduction

Material

- ☐ Lampshade frames in various sizes, obtainable at most handicraft shops.
  Fabric for the lampshade cover
- ☐ Tape measure
- ☐ Six-cord elastic
- ☐ Lace in various widths. Never use synthetic lace on fabric that requires ironing at high temperatures, as this kind of lace may melt.
- ☐ Decorative cord, satin ribbon, binding and fabric inserts
- ☐ Handembroidery thread
- ☐ Machine embroidery thread
- ☐ Various kinds of needles and sufficient of each e.g. embroidery needles; one with a narrow eye for stitching beads; and one with a blunt point for threading elastic.
- ☐ Three kinds of scissors: a good, sharp pair for cutting fabric; a pair for cutting paper; and a pair with sharp points for embroidery.
- ☐ Rustproof pins
- ☐ Vanishing ink to mark guidelines: do not use this if you are not going to complete the work in one sitting, as the marks will disappear. There is a blue marking pen available with ink that does not disappear, but has to be washed out later.
- ☐ Crochet thread or thin string
- ☐ Ruler
- ☐ Pencil
- ☐ Tracing paper
- ☐ Filling for clown

Hints

Sewing machine

Modern sewing machines have double needles and decorative stitches which may be used to make an interesting lampshade, but even with the simplest machine it is still possible to make a beautiful lampshade. Simply substitute fancy ribbons, cords and lace for the decorative stitches to achieve a similar effect.

With an overlock machine you can achieve professional finishes. If you do not own an overlock machine, finish off with a zigzag or similar stitch. Make sure that the inside or wrong side of the lampshade is neat and that all stitching is worked away and ended off neatly.

Fabric

- ☐ Choose fabric that blends in with the atmosphere of the room.
- ☐ Make allowance for repeat patterns when buying fabric, as you may have to join fabric with some of the lampshades.
- ☐ Fabrics in lighter shades let bright light through, while dark and densely woven fabrics let through less light.
- ☐ You may use different fabric textures in a lampshade cover, e.g. floral or printed cotton with a plain glazed cotton frill.
- ☐ The fabric should preferably be washable.
- ☐ Shrink all fabrics before sewing.
- ☐ The elasticity of fabrics varies. Stretch your chosen fabric around the frame and compare the measurements with those of the pattern. If necessary, make it wider, longer or shorter according to the elasticity of the fabric.

Frills

- ☐ It is better not to use thick, densely woven fabrics for frills, since this causes thick seams and makes gathering difficult.
- ☐ Gather frills fully.
- ☐ Using zigzag stitches over a piece of crochet thread or thin string makes it easier to draw in and gather a frill neatly. Stitch the string at the beginning with a narrow stitch and keep it taut while stitching. You can even out the gathers by hand afterwards.
- ☐ To gather a frill, sew two rows of basting stitches or use a gathering foot.

Sewing thread

- ☐ Use good quality sewing thread
- ☐ With DMC machine embroidery thread, you can achieve a neat raised effect, especially with fancy stitches.
- ☐ Use DMC stranded embroidery thread for cross-stitch and other embroidery.

Basic lampshade

METHOD

- ☐ Lampshade frames with the same diameter do not necessarily have the same circumference. Measure each frame before you begin making the cover.
- ☐ Measure the circumference and the height of the frame.
- ☐ Cut a strip of fabric: circumference + 3 cm seam allowance (Sketch 1a, point 1) x height + 8 cm seam allowance (Sketch 1a, point 2) for the top and the bottom. The 3 cm seam allowance is quite wide but it is better to cut off an extra centimetre or two than to end up with a cover that is too narrow.
- ☐ Mark or iron in a guideline approximately 6–8 cm from the bottom of the fabric (Sketch 1a, point 3).

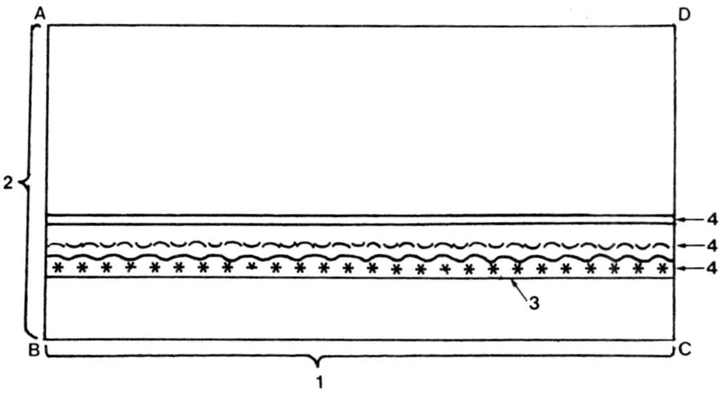

Sketch 1a

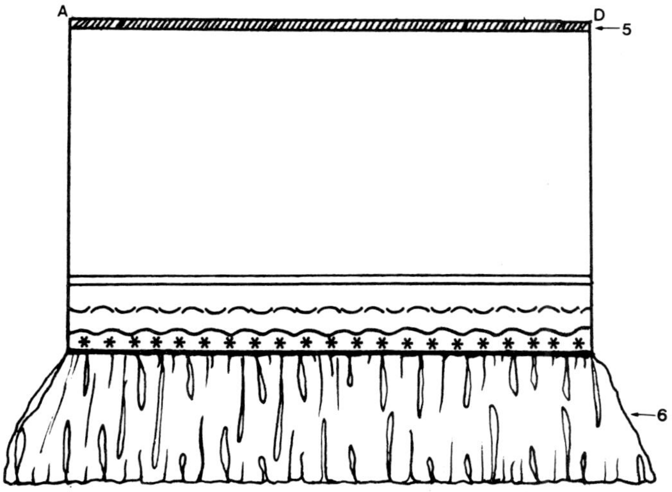

Sketch 1b

- ☐ Stitch lace, ribbon, decorative cord, etc. above this line (Sketch 1a, point 4).
- ☐ Pin the side seams of the fabric, making sure that the ribbons, stitches, lace, tucks, inserts and decorative cord correspond.
- ☐ Stitch the side seams together.
- ☐ Finish off this side seam.
- ☐ Finish off the top and the bottom of the fabric, and fold 1 cm casings over to the wrong side.
- ☐ Stitch the casings (top and bottom), leaving openings for inserting the elastic (Sketch 1b, point 5).
- ☐ Gather or pleat the finished frill to match the measurements of the fabric exactly; stitch the side seam.
- ☐ Stitch the frill just below the marked line (Sketch 1b, point 6).
- ☐ Sew on beads and ribbons, if appropriate. (In some cases you can stitch the ribbon along the stitching line of the frill.)
- ☐ Thread the six-cord elastic through the top and the bottom, but do not cut it.
- ☐ Pull the cover over the frame.
- ☐ Make sure that the side seam lies over one of the supporting wires of the frame.
- ☐ Pull both pieces of elastic tight, and knot them a few times.
- ☐ Cut off the excess elastic and put it aside for later use.
- ☐ Sew up the two openings for the elastic by hand.

Dainty in lace and stripes

MATERIALS

Frame for ceiling lamp: diameter 41 cm
Striped cotton fabric: 1,35 m x 45 cm
Cream-coloured cotton lace: 1,35 m x 9 cm
2 cm cream-coloured decorative cord: 1,35 m long
Cream-coloured cotton lace for frill: 2,80 m x 9 cm
Ordinary machine thread
Card of six-cord elastic

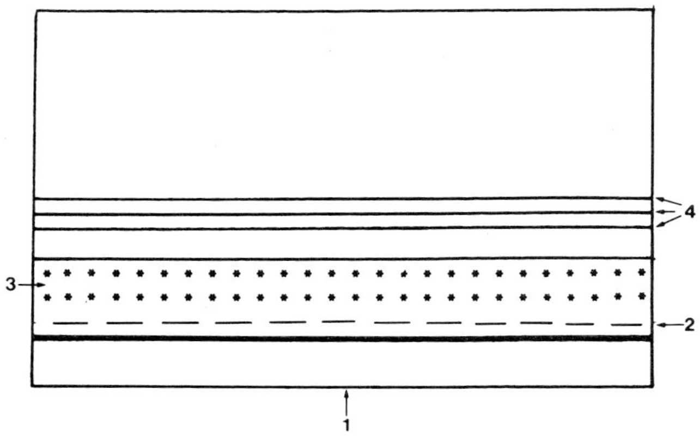

Sketch 2a

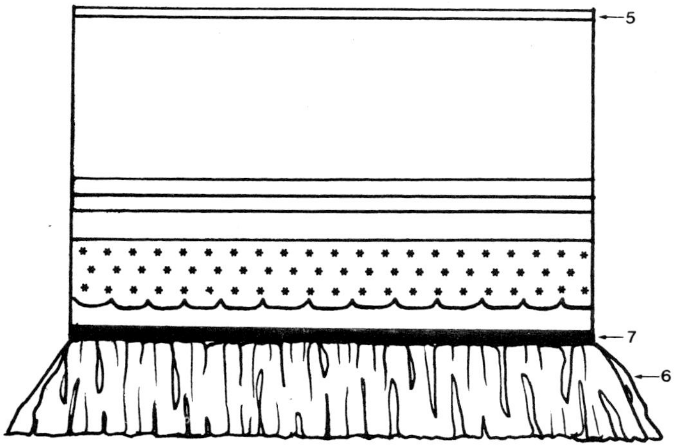

Sketch 2b

METHOD

- Finish off the bottom raw edge of the striped fabric (Sketch 2a, point 1). Mark or iron in a guideline 10 cm from the finished edge (Sketch 2a, point 2). Place the bottom edge of the cream-coloured cotton lace on the guideline and stitch down using honeycomb or a similar stitch (Sketch 2a, point 3). Stitch the other edge higher up, also with honeycomb stitch. Now cut away the fabric behind the cotton lace. The honeycomb stitch will prevent the fabric from unravelling when you cut it away.
- Stitch three 5 mm tucks, facing down and 1 cm apart, 2 cm above the stitched cotton lace (Sketch 2a, point 4).
- Wrap the strip of fabric which you have finished decorating, right side facing in, around the frame. Pin the side seam, making sure that the fabric fits snugly around the frame. Make sure that all stitching, lace, etc. correspond exactly at the seam.
- Remove the fabric from the frame and stitch the side seam with double stitches. It has to be taut when you pull it over the frame and there will be a lot of tension on the seam. Finish off the seam.
- Finish off the top raw edge and fold a 1 cm casing over to the inside - it must be broad enough for the elastic to pass through (Sketch 2b, point 5). Stitch with a straight stitch, leaving an opening for inserting the elastic. Repeat at the bottom of the fabric.
- Join the cotton lace of the frill (Sketch 2b, point 6), and gather it evenly to fit the fabric exactly. Stitch the frill onto the fabric with criss-cross stitches 5 cm from the edge of the fabric. Now sew on the decorative cord along the top edge of the stitched frill (Sketch 2b, point 7).
- Thread the six-cord elastic through the top and the bottom casings. Pull the cover over the frame, making sure that the seam lies directly over one of the supporting wires of the frame.
- Pull both elastics tight. Knot the elastic a few times, and cut off the excess elastic a small distance from the knots. Sew up the openings by hand.

Ducklings on a roundabout

MATERIALS

Frame for a table lamp: diameter 36 cm
Floral cotton fabric: 1,21 m x 20 cm
Matching cotton insert: 1,21 m x 12 cm
Floral cotton fabric: 1,21 x 8 cm
Floral cotton fabric for frill: 2,20 m x 9 cm
Yellow anglaise cotton lace: 2,20 m x 4,5 cm
8 mm light blue satin ribbon: 4,62 m long
6 mm yellow satin ribbon: 2,42 m long
Blue and yellow machine thread
Card of six-cord elastic

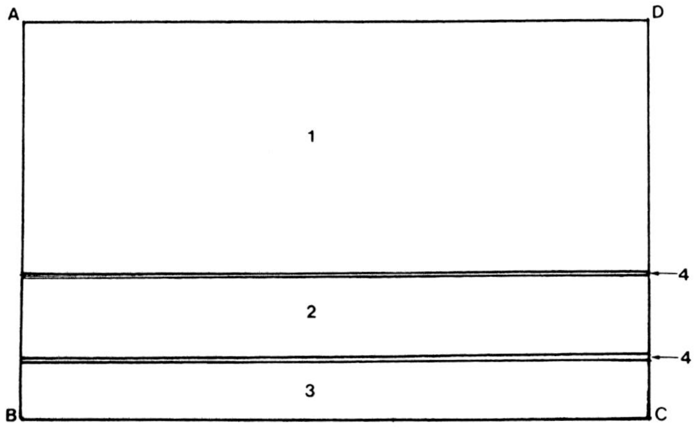

Sketch 3a

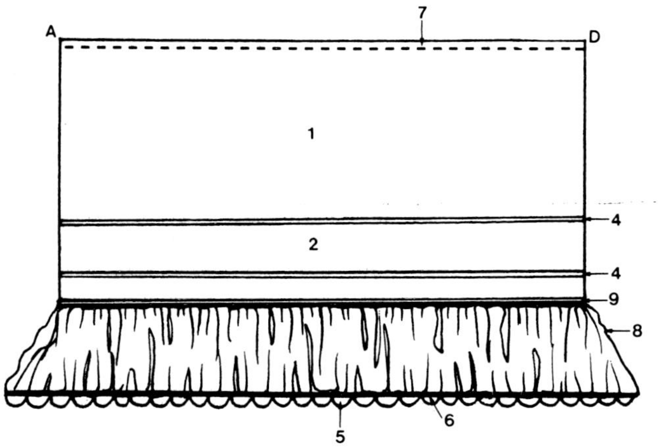

Sketch 3b

METHOD

- ☐ Neatly finish off both long edges of the 1,21 m x 20 cm fabric strip (AD and BC). Repeat with the cotton insert and the other floral fabric strip.
- ☐ When using an insert with repeat patterns, as in this case, make sure that the pattern fits exactly around the frame. Choose inserts with care so that you do not have to remove too much from the pattern. Make tiny tucks in the floral part of the insert if it is too long.
- ☐ Join the three parts by overlapping them slightly and then stitching with criss-cross stitch (Sketch 3a, points 1, 2 and 3). Now stitch the yellow satin ribbon over these stitches at the top and the bottom of the insert (Sketch 3a, point 4).
- ☐ Wrap the joined piece of fabric, right side facing in, around the frame, and pin the side seam. Make sure that the yellow satin ribbons correspond and that the fabric fits snugly around the frame.
- ☐ Stitch the side seam with a double action stitch and finish off neatly. Stitch two 1 cm casings (Sketch 3b, point 7) for threading the elastic at the top and the bottom edges of the fabric, leaving openings for inserting the elastic.
- ☐ Complete the frill by first finishing off both long raw edges. Using criss-cross stitch, stitch the yellow cotton lace along one edge (Sketch 3b, point 5). Stitch some of the blue satin ribbon over the criss-cross stitches (Sketch 3b, point 6). Sew up the side seam and gather the frill evenly to fit the completed fabric part.
- ☐ Pin the frill (Sketch 3b, point 8) 2,5 cm from the yellow satin ribbon. Using criss-cross stitch, stitch blue satin ribbons one above the other over the top edge of the frill (Sketch 3b, point 9).
- ☐ Thread elastic through the top and the bottom casings, and pull the fabric over the frame. Make sure that the side seam lies over one of the supporting wires of the frame.
- ☐ Pull the top and the bottom elastic tight to stretch the fabric taut over the frame. Knot the elastic a few times, and cut off the excess elastic a small distance from the knot.
- ☐ For additional decoration, sew a bow onto the fabric.
- ☐ Press the frill open, and place the completed article on a pretty stand.

Paisley pleasure

MATERIALS

Frame for table lamp: diameter 36 cm
Cotton fabric with paisley design: 1,21 m x 40 cm
Pink glazed cotton for frill: 2,20 m x 10 cm
Cream-coloured cotton lace: 2,20 m x 9 cm
14 mm wine-red satin ribbon: 2,20 m long
2 cm pink decorative cord: 2,12 m long
6 mm pink satin ribbon: 1,21 m long
8 pearl beads
Pink and wine-red machine thread
Card of six-cord elastic

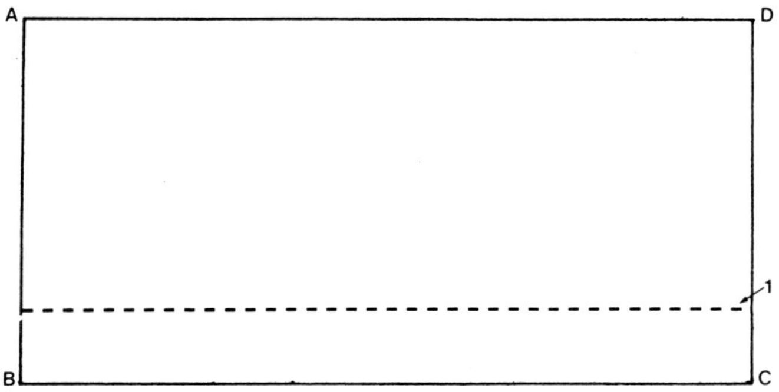

Sketch 4a

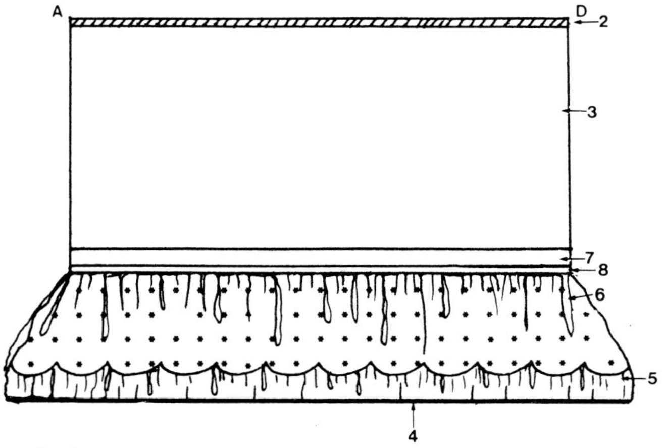

Sketch 4b

METHOD

- ☐ Finish off the raw edges of the two long sides (AD and BC). Mark or iron in a guideline 8 cm from line BC to help you when you sew the frill on (Sketch 4a, point 1). Wrap the fabric (Sketch 4b, point 3), right side facing in, around the frame. Stretch until taut, and pin the side seam.
- ☐ Stitch the side seam with a double action stitch, and finish it off. Press the seam flat.
- ☐ Using straight stitch, stitch 1 cm casings at the top and the bottom for threading the elastic (Sketch 4b, point 2).
- ☐ Finish off both raw edges of the glazed cotton frill (Sketch 4b, point 5). Using criss-cross stitches, stitch the wine-red satin ribbon onto one finished-off edge (Sketch 4b, point 4). Place the cotton lace over the right side of the pink glazed cotton frill strip (Sketch 4b, point 6). The scalloped edge of the cotton lace must face down, i.e. towards the wine-red satin ribbon. Now gather the glazed cotton strip and the cotton lace at the same time until they fit exactly around the completed fabric. Finish off the side seam, and place the frill over the guideline. Arrange the gathers evenly, and stitch the frill.
- ☐ Stitch the pink satin ribbon, using a criss-cross stitch, over this row of stitches (Sketch 4b, point 8). Make sure that the beginning and the end of the ribbon meet at the side seam of the fabric. Now stitch the decorative cord directly above the satin ribbon (Sketch 4b, point 7). Again make sure that the beginning and the end meet at the side seam.
- ☐ Thread the elastic through the top and the bottom casings. Pull the cover over the frame, making sure that the seam lies over a supporting wire of the frame. Pull both pieces of elastic tight so that the cover fits snugly around the frame. Make a few knots and cut the excess elastic a small distance from the knots. Sew up the two openings by hand.
- ☐ Space the pearl beads on the decorative cord, and sew them on.
- ☐ Pull the cover over the frame.

Striking in taffeta

MATERIALS

Frame for table lamp: diameter 36 cm
Black watered tafetta or similar fabric: 1,21 m x 40 cm
Black watered tafetta for frill: 2,50 m x 10 cm
5 mm gold decorative cord: 2,50 m long
1,5 cm gold and black decorative cord: 1,21 m long
Black machine thread
Card of six-cord elastic

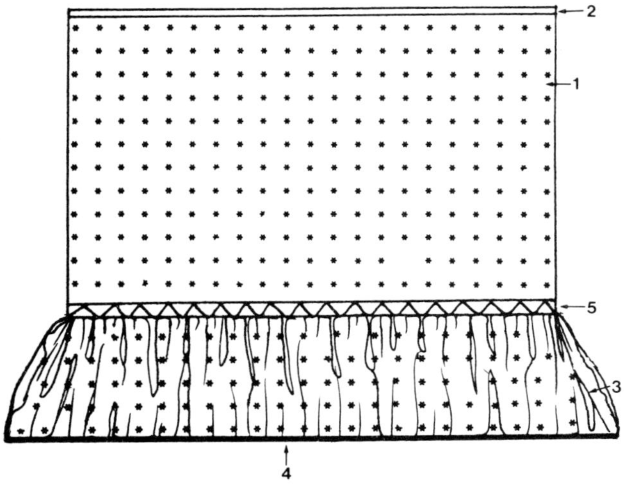

Sketch 5

METHOD

- ☐ Finish off the two raw edges of the large piece of watered taffeta (Sketch 5, point 1). Mark or iron in a guideline about 8 cm from line BC for stitching the frill.
- ☐ Wrap the fabric, right side facing in, around the frame. Pull the fabric taut while pinning the side seam. Remove the fabric, and stitch the side seam with a double action straight stitch. Finish off the raw edge and press the side seam open.
- ☐ Finish off the two raw edges of the frill, and stitch the gold decorative cord onto one finished edge (Sketch 5, point 4).
- ☐ Gather the frill until it fits neatly over the taffeta cover. Stitch the side seam of the frill, and finish off the raw edge.
- ☐ Using criss-cross stitch, stitch the gathered frill onto the right side of the cover along the guideline. Make sure that the side seam of the frill corresponds with that of the cover. Stitch on the gold and black decorative cord with two rows of straight stitches over the criss-cross stitches (Sketch 5, point 5).
- ☐ Stitch two 1 cm casings at the top and the bottom of the cover (Sketch 5, point 2), leaving openings for inserting the elastic.
- ☐ Thread the elastic through the casings. Pull the cover over the frame, making sure that the side seam lies over one of the supporting wires of the frame. Pull both pieces of elastic tight so that the cover fits snugly around the frame. Make a few knots and cut the excess elastic a small distance from the knots. Sew up the openings for the elastic by hand.
- ☐ Arrange the frill evenly, and place the lampshade on a stand.

Embroider a posy

MATERIALS

Frame for table lamp: diameter 46 cm
White cotton fabric: 1,55 m x 46 cm
White lining fabric: 1,55 m x 46 cm
White anglaise lace: 2,80 m x 11 cm
Narrow cotton lace insert: 1,55 m x 3 cm
8 mm light pink satin ribbon: 3,10 m long
8 mm light blue satin ribbon: 1,55 m long
DMC stranded embroidery thread: 775; 523; 502; 778; 211;
340; 745 and 776 (one strand of each)
Purple and pink DMC machine embroidery thread
Ordinary machine thread
8 mm pink, light blue and light purple satin ribbon, each 1,60 m long
Card of six-cord elastic
Embroidery needle
Embroidery frame

METHOD

- Divide the white fabric as in Sketch 6a. Draw the flower design 9 cm from line BC at the three marked places. First finish off the raw edges AD and BC to prevent them from unravelling while you embroider.
- Follow the embroidery diagram. The small lines indicate the direction of the stitches.
- When you have embroidered the designs, place the lining fabric at the back of the white cotton with the embroidery. Make sure that you have worked away all the loose threads. Catch the two pieces of fabric at AD and BC. The pieces must lie smoothly on top of each other.
- Mark or iron in a guideline 5 cm above the embroidery (Sketch 6a, point 1). With the purple machine embroidery thread, stitch a row of decorative stitches along this line. Using criss-cross stitch, stitch the blue satin ribbon 1 cm higher up (Sketch 6a, point 2). With honeycomb or a similar stitch, stitch the lace insert right next to the blue satin ribbon (Sketch 6a, point 3).
- Stitch a row of dense satin stitches with the pink machine embroidery thread along the edge of the lace (Sketch 6a, point 4). Using criss-cross stitches, stitch the pink satin ribbon above the lace insert (Sketch 6a, point 5).
- Mark or iron in a guideline for the frill, 2 cm below the embroidery (Sketch 6a, point 6).
- Wrap the fabric, right side facing in, around the frame. Make sure that all the ribbons and the lace correspond, and pin the side seams. Stitch the side seam with a double action straight stitch, and finish off the raw edge of the seam.
- Stitch 1 cm casings at the top and the bottom edges of the cover, leaving two openings for inserting the elastic.
- Stitch the white anglaise lace frill along the guideline, forming box pleats as you go. Make sure that the side seams of the lace and the cover correspond.
- With criss-cross stitch, stitch the pink satin ribbon 5 mm from the top of the white anglaise lace (Sketch 6b, point 8). Divide the 1,60 m piece of ribbon into three equal lengths. Make a bow with each of the three colours, and stitch the three bows onto the pink satin ribbon (Sketch 6b, point 9).
- Thread the elastic through the casings. Pull the cover over the frame, making sure that the side seam lies over one of the supporting wires of the frame. Pull both pieces of elastic tight so that the cover fits snugly around the frame. Make a few knots and cut the excess elastic a small distance from the knots. Sew up the openings for the elastic by hand.
- Arrange the frill evenly and place the lampshade on a suitable stand.

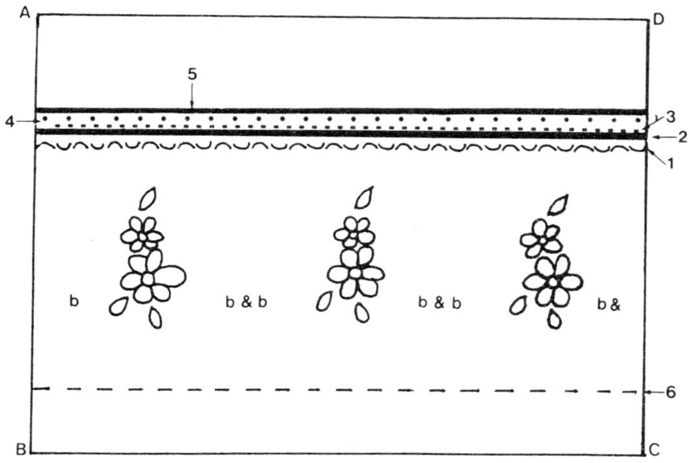

Sketch 6a

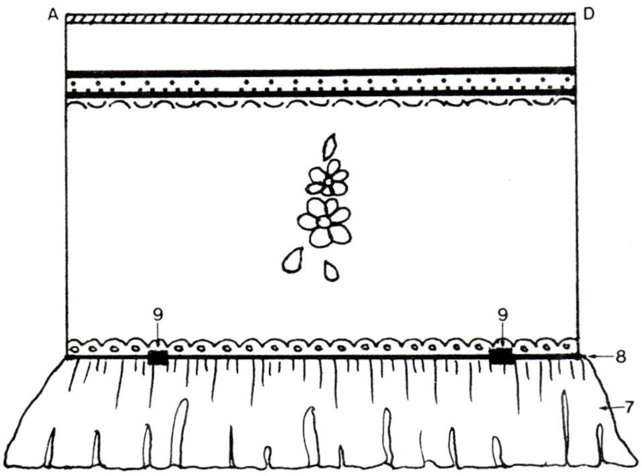

Sketch 6b

DMC

*	775
s	340
+	523
dark parts	745
v	211
●	776
o	778
stems and large leaf	502

All the stitches are embroidered in satin stitch, except the stems and stalks, which are embroidered in stem stitch. Enlarge the above diagram by 32% to actual size.

Lace elegance

MATERIALS

Frame for table lamp: diameter 31 cm
White fabric: 1,07 m x 36 cm
White lace: 1,07 m x 11 cm
White lace with long points: 1,07 m x 22 cm
2 cm white lace insert: 1,07 m long
3,5 cm white lace insert: 1,07 m long
10 mm white satin ribbon: 1,07 m long
19 pearl buttons
10 tear drop buttons
Blue and white machine embroidery thread
Ordinary white machine thread
Card of six-cord elastic
Thin needle

METHOD

- Finish off the raw edges of the two long sides (AD and BC) of the white fabric. Mark or iron in a guideline 5 cm from the bottom of the fabric (Sketch 7, point 1).
- Using honeycomb stitch, stitch the 11 cm wide white lace 1 cm from this line (Sketch 7, point 2). Stitch both sides of the lace. Cut away the fabric behind the lace.
- Stitch the 10 mm wide white satin ribbon 1 cm above the lace (Sketch 7, point 3). Stitch a row of decorative stitches with white machine embroidery thread 1 cm higher (Sketch 7, point 4). Stitch the 2 cm wide lace insert 0,5 cm above the decorative stitches (Sketch 7, point 5).
- With blue embroidery thread, stitch a row of decorative stitches 1 cm above the insert (Sketch 7, point 6). Leaving 1 cm open, stitch two pin tucks (Sketch 7, point 7). Leaving 0,5 cm open, stitch the 3,5 cm wide lace insert onto the fabric with honeycomb stitch (Sketch 7, point 8). Cut away the fabric strip behind the lace insert. Stitch a row of blue decorative stitches 1 cm above this insert (Sketch 7, point 9).
- Wrap the decorated piece of fabric, right side facing in, around the frame. Make sure that all lace, ribbon and stitches correspond exactly, and pin the side seam. Stitch the side seam with a double action straight stitch, and finish off the raw edge. Press the seam open.
- Stitch 1 cm casings at the top and the bottom of the fabric for threading the elastic.
- Join the side seam of the pointed lace as invisably as possible, making sure that that you do not alter the point pattern.
- Stitch the pointed lace along the guideline (Sketch 7, point 1). The join in the lace must correspond with the side seam of the cover.
- Now sew on all the pearl buttons at the marked places (Sketch 7, point 10), and then the teardrop buttons on the bottom edge of the pointed lace.
- Thread the elastic through the casings and stretch the cover over the frame. Make sure that the side seam lies over one of the supporting wires of the frame.
- Pull the elastic taut, knot it a few times and cut the excess elastic a small distance from the buttons.
- Place the completed lampshade on a suitable stand.

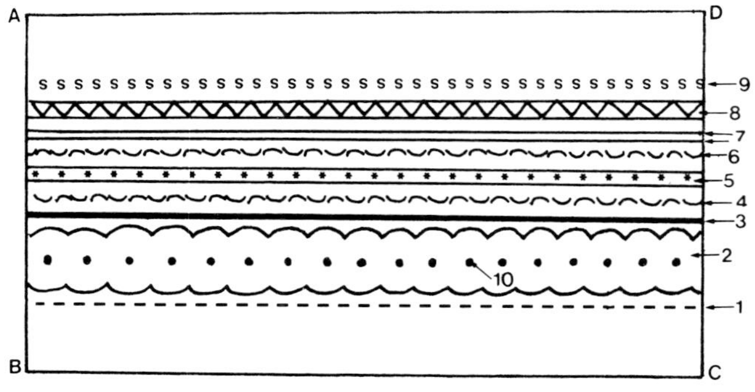

Sketch 7

Spring fantasy

MATERIALS

Frame for ceiling lamp: diameter 51 cm
Granny print cotton fabric: 1,7 m x 51 cm
Granny print cotton fabric (frill): 3 m x 8 cm
1,5 cm blue cotton lace: 6,52 m long
3 cm blue anglaise lace: 4,76 m long
Cream-coloured cotton lace: 1,76 m x 11 cm
8 mm apricot satin ribbon: 3,52 m long
Ordinary machine thread
Card of six-cord elastic

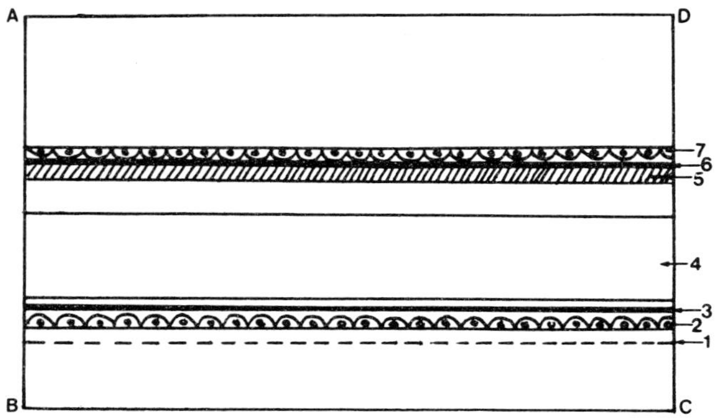

Sketch 8a

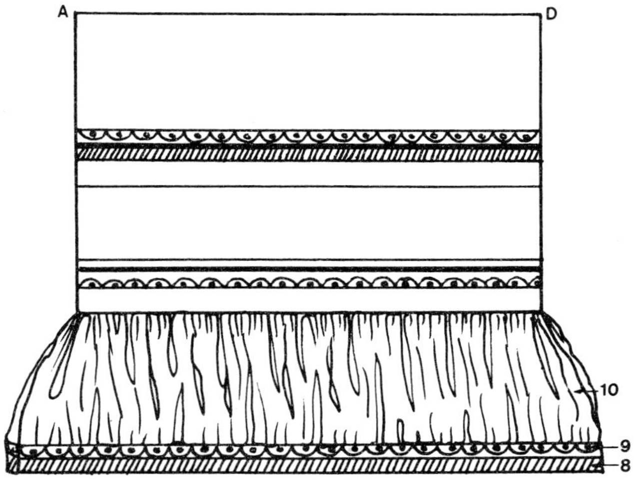

Sketch 8b

METHOD

- ☐ Finish off the raw edges of the strip of Granny print cotton fabric. Mark or iron in a guideline for the frill, 7 cm from line BC (Sketch 8a, point 1).
- ☐ Leave 1 cm open above this line and stitch the 1,5 cm wide blue cotton lace onto the material, using zigzag stitches (Sketch 8a, point 2). Stitch the apricot satin ribbon directly above the lace (Sketch 8a, point 3).
- ☐ With honeycomb stitch, stitch both sides of the broad cream-coloured lace onto the fabric above the satin ribbon (Sketch 8a, point 4). Cut away the fabric behind the lace.
- ☐ Leaving 5 cm open, stitch the top of the broad blue anglaise cotton lace (Sketch 8a, point 5). The scalloped edge of this lace must face downwards. Stitch the apricot satin ribbon just above this lace (Sketch 8a, point 6).
- ☐ Stitch the narrow, blue cotton lace above the ribbon with the scalloped edge downwards (Sketch 8a, point 7).
- ☐ Stretch the fabric, right side facing in, around the frame. Make sure that all the decorations correspond, and pin the side seam. Stitch the side seam with double action straight stitch. Finish off the raw edge of the seam, and press the seam open.
- ☐ Stitch 1 cm casings at the top and the bottom of the cover, leaving openings for inserting the elastic.
- ☐ Finish off the two long sides of the frill strip (Sketch 8b, point 10), and stitch the broad blue anglaise lace onto the one edge (Sketch 8b, point 8). Stitch the narrow blue lace directly above the broad lace (Sketch 8b, point 9). Fold the other side of the frill over 0,5 cm and stitch the hem. Fold even box pleats into this side, then stitch it onto the fabric along the guideline with a row of criss-cross stitches. Make sure that the joining seam of the frill corresponds with the side seam.
- ☐ Thread the elastic through the two casings, and stretch the cover carefully over the frame, especially the lace strip that does not have a fabric backing. Make sure that the side seam lies over a supporting wire of the frame. Pull the two pieces of elastic tight until the cover fits snugly over the frame.
- ☐ Knot the elastic a few times, and cut the excess elastic a small distance from the knots. Sew up both openings by hand, and hang the lampshade up.

Light up with lustre

MATERIALS

Frame for table lamp: diameter 36 cm
Black and pink floral cotton fabric: 1,21 m x 40 cm
Light pink glazed cotton: 2,50 m x 10,5 cm
White cotton lace insert: 2,05 cm x 3,5 cm
6 mm black satin ribbon: 5 m long
6 mm pink satin ribbon: 2,85 m long
Pink machine embroidery thread
Black and pink ordinary machine thread
Card of six-cord elastic

METHOD

- When making this cover you need to keep your wits about you, and you must have an accurate eye. First finish off the raw edges of the two long sides of the floral fabric (Sketch 9a, AD and BC).
- Mark or iron in a guideline 9 cm from line BC (Sketch 9a, point 1). Stitch the white lace insert 4 cm higher up with dense criss-cross stitches and pink thread (Sketch 9a, point 2). Carefully cut away the fabric behind the lace.
- Wrap the fabric, right side facing in, around the frame. Pull it taut and pin the side seam. Now stitch the side seam with an ordinary stitch and press the seam flat (Sketch 9d, point 10).
- Turn the fabric right side out. Place some of the white lace exactly over the side seam (Sketches 9a, 9c and 9d, point 3). Stitch both sides with a row of honeycomb stitches and cut away the fabric of the side seam behind the lace. Using criss-cross stitches and pink thread, stitch the pink satin ribbon onto the sides of the white lace (Sketches 9a, 9c and 9d, point 4).
- Place the cover fabric in front of you, as indicated in Sketch 9c, and do exactly the same with the side opposite the vertical lace insert (Sketch 9c, point 9).
- Finish off both long sides of the strip of pink glazed cotton with a row of dense pink satin stitches (Sketch 9b, point 5). Stitch the black satin ribbon 1 cm from one of the finished edges. Leave 0,5 cm open, and then stitch more black satin ribbon on (Sketch 9b, point 7).
- Join the side seam of the frill strip, and finish off the raw edge – a French seam looks very neat.
- Gather the frill and arrange neatly. Stitch the frill along the guideline (Sketches 9a, 9c and 9d, point 1), but allow 1 cm of the top of the frill to extend beyond the line (Sketch 9b, point 11). Using criss-cross stitches, stitch some of the pink satin ribbon over the previous stitching (Sketch 9b, point 8). Make sure that the beginning and the end correspond with that of the frill.
- Again finish off the top and the bottom sides that you finished off before, this time including the edges of the lace inserts (Sketch 9a, AD and BC).
- Fold 1 cm casings at the top and the bottom of the fabric and stitch, leaving openings for inserting the elastic (Sketch 9b, point 6).
- Thread elastic through and place the cover over the frame. Make sure that the two lace inserts lie over two supporting wires of the frame. Pull the two pieces of elastic tight until the cover fits snugly over the frame. Knot the elastic a few times when the fabric is stretched taut, and cut off the excess elastic. Sew up the two openings and even out the frill.

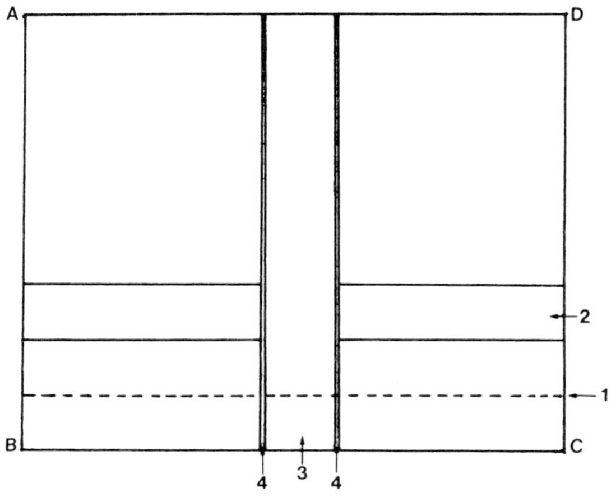

Sketch 9a

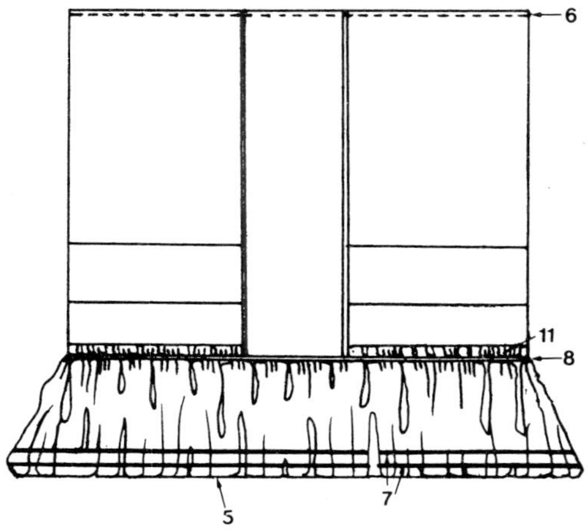

Sketch 9b

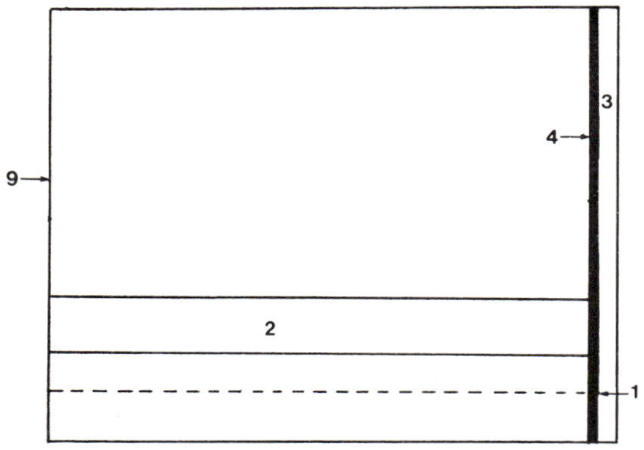

Sketch 9c

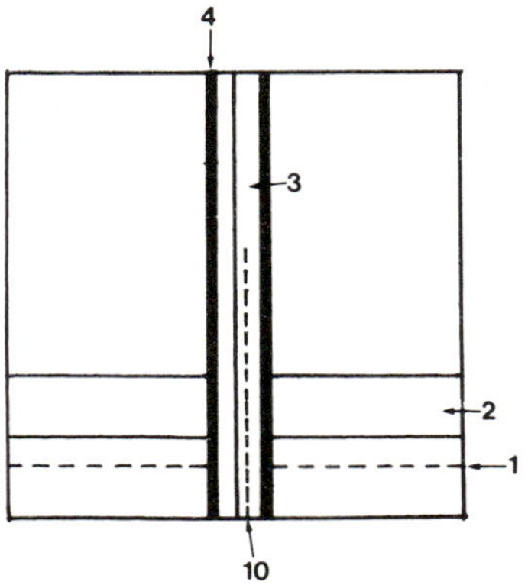

Sketch 9d

Striking strips

MATERIALS

Frame for table lamp: diameter 46 cm
3 pieces of floral fabric: each 31 cm x 46 cm
3 pieces of pink glazed cotton: each 22 cm x 46 cm
Pink glazed cotton for frill: 2,8 m x 10 cm
8 mm blue satin ribbon: 2,8 m long
8 mm mauve satin ribbon: 2,8 m long
10 mm mauve satin ribbon: 1,55 m long
Blue and pink machine thread
Card of six-cord elastic

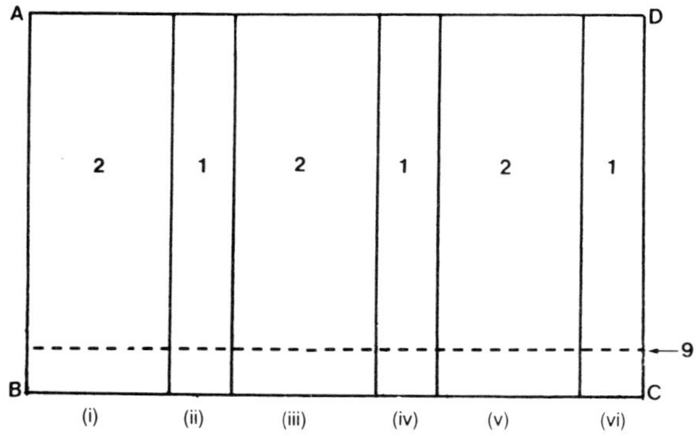

Sketch 10a

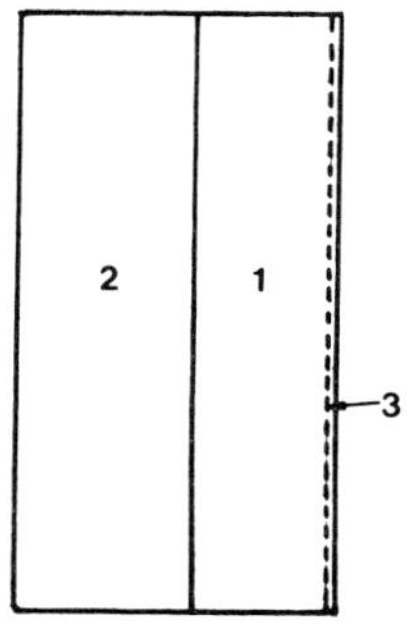

Sketch 10b

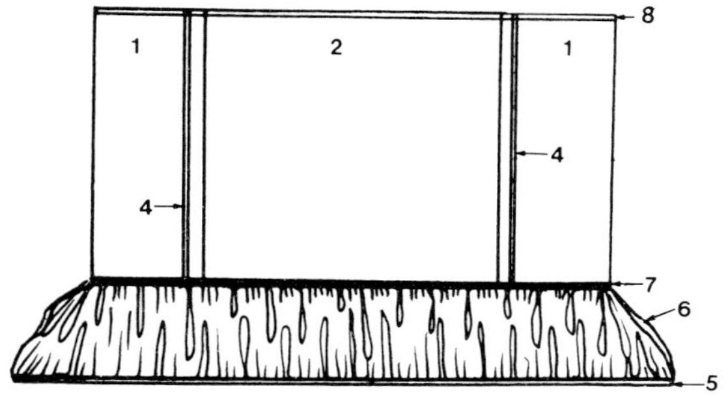

Sketch 10c

METHOD

- ☐ With this lampshade, you will be stitching six pieces of fabric together. Place one of the pink glazed cotton pieces over a piece of floral fabric, right sides together (Sketch 10b).
- ☐ Stitch a row of double action straight stitches 0,5 cm from the edge (Sketch 10b, point 3), and finish off the raw edge. Alternate the fabric pieces and stitch all of them together with a 0,5 cm seam [Sketch 10a, (i) to (vi)]. You now have a continuous piece of fabric. Press all the seams open. Stitch the narrow mauve satin ribbon 0,5 cm inside the pink glazed cotton (Sketch 10c, point 4). Repeat with all the pink strips.
- ☐ Finish off the raw edges of the two long sides of the frill strip (Sketch 10c, point 6). Using criss cross stitch, stitch the blue satin ribbon onto one edge of the frill (Sketch 10c, point 5). Gather the frill strip evenly, and join the side seam. Finish off the seam, and stitch the frill 7 cm from line BC onto the cover (Sketch 10a, point 9).
- ☐ Stitch the broad mauve satin ribbon over the stitching of the frill with two rows of small zigzag stitches (Sketch 10c, point 7).
- ☐ Fold 1 cm casings at the top and the bottom of the cover (Sketch 10c, point 8). Stitch the casings, leaving two openings for inserting the elastic.
- ☐ Thread the elastic through the two casings, and pull the cover over the frame. Pull the two pieces of elastic tight, make sure that the fabric is stretched evenly, and knot the elastic. Cut off the excess elastic, and place your lampshade on a suitable stand.

Hint: All fabrics are not equally elastic, so that the joined cover section (Sketch10a) may be too wide for the frame. In that case, adjust the excess width evenly at the seams (e.g. make each seam 2mm wider).

Hearts in cross-stitch

MATERIALS

Frame for table lamp: diameter 31 cm
Blue fabric: 1,06 m x 36 cm
Blue fabric for frill: 2,2 m x 8 cm
4,5 cm cream-coloured cross-stitch fabric insert: 1,06 m long
4 cm cream-coloured cotton lace: 4,32 m long
6 mm wine-red satin ribbon: 4,32 m long
14 mm wine-red satin ribbon: 1,06 m long
Wine-red, dark blue and cream-coloured machine thread
DMC stranded embroidery thread: 939 (2 strands); 3685 (1 strand)
Embroidery needle
Card of six-cord elastic

METHOD

- ☐ Cover the two cut sides of the cross-stitch insert with cellotape to prevent them from unravelling while you work. Embroider the first heart 10 stitch spaces from the side. Embroider 25 blue hearts and outline them with wine-red thread.
- ☐ Mark or iron in a guideline on the blue fabric 6 cm from the bottom line BC (Sketch 11a, point 1). Stitch the cross-stitch insert 2 cm higher (Sketch 11a, point 2).
- ☐ Leave 1 cm open (Sketch 11a, point 3), and stitch some of the cream-coloured lace on, with the scalloped part pointing down (Sketch 11a, point 4). Use a stitch (e.g. honeycomb stitch) that will prevent the fabric from unravelling when you cut away the material behind the lace later on. Using criss-cross stitches, stitch some of the 6 mm wide satin ribbon along the top edge of the lace (Sketch 11a, point 5).
- ☐ Leave 5 cm open, and stitch more of the cream-coloured lace (Sketch 11a, point 4) and some of the 6 mm satin ribbon on (Sketch 11a, point 5).
- ☐ Carefully cut away the material behind the two lace inserts.
- ☐ Wrap the cover, right side facing in, around the frame. Make sure that the fabric is stretched taut and that all the lace, ribbon, embroidery, etc. correspond before pinning the side seam. Stitch the seam with a double action straight stitch and finish off the raw edge of the seam. Press the seam open.
- ☐ Fold 1 cm casings at the top and the bottom of the cover (Sketch 11b, point 7). Stitch the seams, leaving openings for inserting the elastic.
- ☐ Finish off both long sides of the blue frill strip (Sketch 11b, point 9). Stitch the 6 mm wide satin ribbon onto one edge (Sketch 11b, point 8). Join and finish off the side seam, and gather the frill evenly. Stitch the frill along the guideline (Sketch 11a, point 1). Stitch the gathered cream-coloured lace over the stitching of the frill (Sketch 11b, point 10).
- ☐ Using two rows of straight stitches, stitch the wide satin ribbon above the cream-coloured lace (Sketch 11b, point 11).
- ☐ Thread elastic through the two casings, and pull the cover over the frame. Make sure that the side seam lies over a supporting wire of the frame. Pull the pieces of elastic tight so that the cover is stretched evenly over the frame, and knot. Cut off the excess elastic, and sew up both openings by hand.
- ☐ A wooden stand is very effective with this lampshade and together they make a table lamp which will turn an entrance hall into something special.

Hint: The measurements for frames vary. Make very certain that your cross-stitch fabric fits around the frame (plus seam allowance) before you cut the fabric. It may be necessary to embroider another heart, or to leave one out. Make sure that the pattern fits into the specific measurements, as it should fit around the frame in one piece.

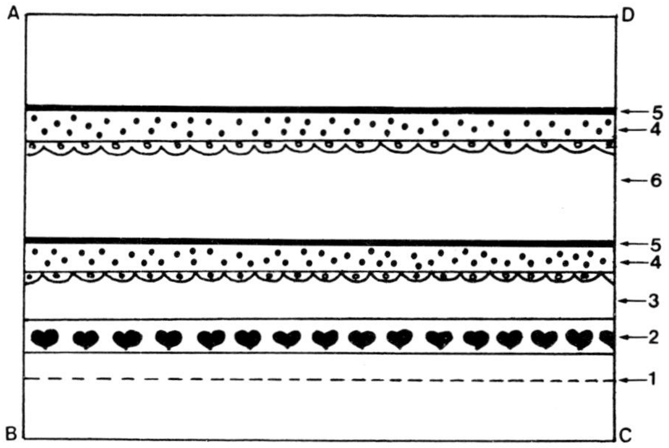

Sketch 11a

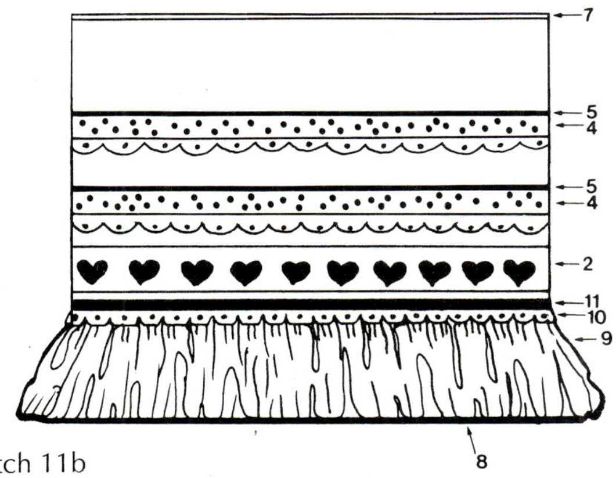

Sketch 11b

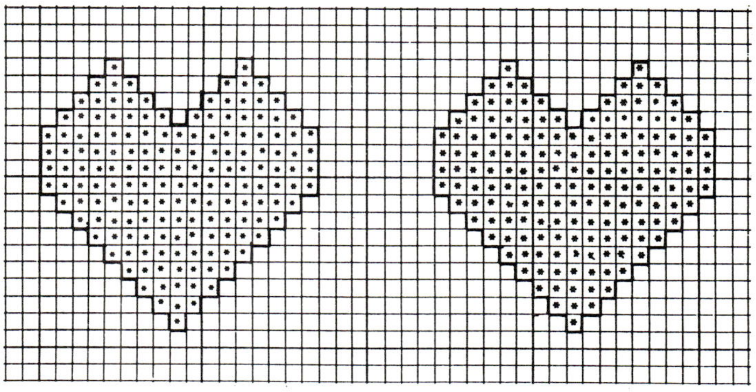

Flights of fancy

MATERIALS

Frame for ceiling lamp: diameter 36 cm
Cream-coloured cotton fabric: 1,21 m x 40 cm
Cream-coloured lace: 3,25 m x 17 cm
12 cream-coloured pearl buttons
8 mm cream-coloured satin ribbon: 2,45 m long
Cream-coloured machine embroidery thread
Cream-coloured machine thread
Card of six-cord elastic

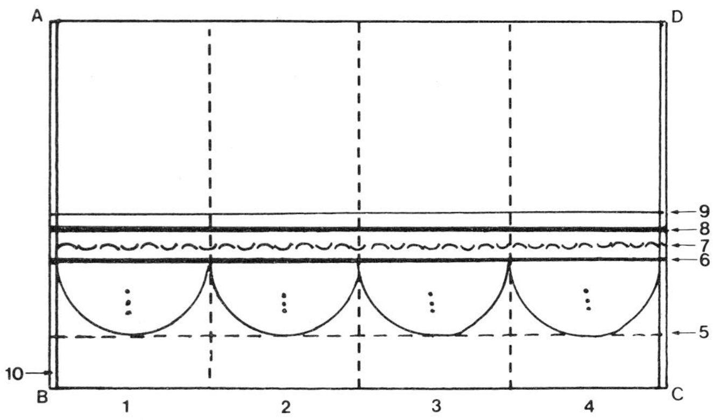

Sketch 12a

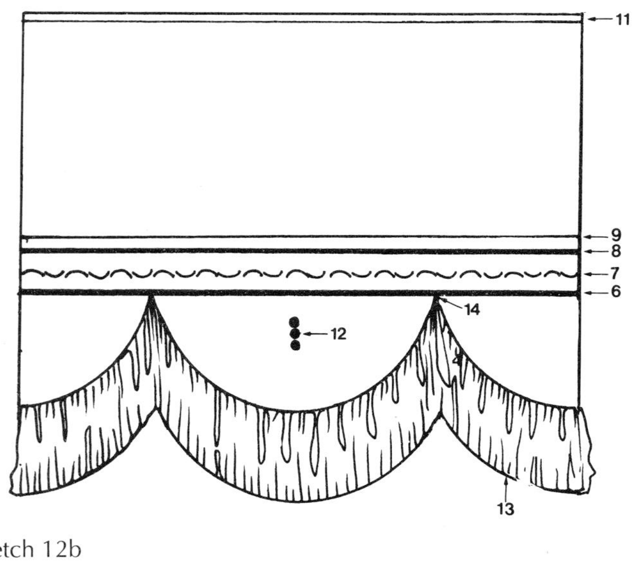

Sketch 12b

METHOD

- Finish off the raw edges of the cream-coloured fabric (AD and BC). Mark or iron in a guideline 5 cm from the bottom of the fabric (Sketch 12a, point 5). Mark or iron in another guideline 10 cm above this line (Sketch 12a, point 6). Fold the fabric into four equally large parts as in Sketch 12a, Blocks 1–4. Do not include the seam allowances (Sketch 12a, point 10).
- Draw four half-circles with a depth of 10 cm in Blocks 1–4; in other words, between the two guidelines. Stitch a strip of satin ribbon along the top guideline (Sketch 12a and 12b, point 6). Leave 0,5 cm open and stitch a row of decorative stitches with the machine embroidery thread (Sketch 12a and 12b, point 7). Stitch more satin ribbon 0,5 cm higher up (Sketches 12a and 12b, point 8). Leaving 1 cm open, stitch a tuck with a depth of 0,5 cm (Sketches 12a and 12b, point 9).
- Wrap the fabric, right side facing in, around the frame. Make sure that the fabric is stretched taut and that all the ribbon, tucks, etc. correspond before pinning the side seam. Stitch the side seam with a double action straight stitch. Finish off the raw edge, and press the side seam open.
- Stitch 1 cm casings at the top and the bottom of the fabric, leaving openings for inserting the elastic (Sketch 12b, point 11).
- Place the fabric right side out in front of you on the work surface. Join the long strip of lace, gathering it very fully. Stitch this lace onto the half-circles (Sketch 12b, point 13). Leave sufficient fullness at the points where the circles meet (Sketch 12b, point 14).
- Sew on the pearl beads at the marked places (Sketch 12b, point 12).
- Thread elastic through both casings, and pull the cover over the frame. Make sure that the side seam lies over a supporting wire of the frame. Pull both pieces of elastic tight, and knot. Cut off the excess elastic, and sew up the openings by hand.

Clowning around

MATERIALS

Frame for ceiling lamp: diameter 51 cm
Red fabric: 1,73 m x 48 cm
Yellow fabric for frill: 3 m x 11 cm
6 mm yellow satin ribbon: 1,73 m long
10 mm blue satin ribbon: 3 m long
6 mm green satin ribbon: 3 m long
3 cm green decorative cord with fringing: 1,75 m long
3 clowns
Card of six-cord elastic
Machine thread: red, blue, yellow and green

Sketch 13a

METHOD

- ☐ Finish off the raw edges of the two long sides of the piece of red fabric. Mark or iron in a guideline 7 cm from the bottom of the fabric. Stitch the yellow satin ribbon on with criss-cross stitches, 1 cm above this line (Sketch 13a, point 1).
- ☐ Wrap the piece of fabric around the frame, right side facing in. Make sure the fabric is stretched taut and that the ribbon corresponds when you pin the side seam. Stitch the side seam, using double action straight stitches. Finish off the raw edge and press the seam open.
- ☐ Make two 1 cm casings at the top and the bottom of the fabric, leaving two openings for inserting the elastic (Sketch 13a, point 2).
- ☐ Finish off the two long sides of the yellow strip of fabric, and stitch the green satin ribbon onto one side, using criss-cross stitches (Sketch 13a, point 3). Stitch on the blue satin ribbon in the same way, 0,5 cm higher (Sketch 13a, point 4). Gather the frill evenly, and join the side seam. Stitch the frill along the guideline. Stitch the green decorative cord with fringing along this row of stitches (Sketch 13a, point 5).
- ☐ Thread elastic through both seams, and pull the cover over the frame. Pull both pieces of elastic tight, and knot a few times. Cut off the excess elastic, and sew up the openings.
- ☐ Sew the clowns onto the shade equally far apart (Sketch 13a, point 6). Remember to remove them when washing the cover.

Clown

MATERIALS

Floral fabric
Plain fabric
Flesh-coloured, elastic fabric
Different coloured satin ribbons
Felt for hands and feet
Red and black marking pen
Yellow wool
Filling

METHOD

- ☐ Trace the pattern onto tracing paper. The patterns in Sketches 13c, 13d and 13e have to be enlarged by 16% to actual size.
- ☐ Cut out the paper patterns, and arrange all the pattern pieces on the fabric. Cut the fabric.
- ☐ Finish off the raw edges of the fabric for the head (Sketch 13e).
- ☐ With strong thread, baste around the head fabric (Sketch 13e, point 1).
- ☐ Fill the head tightly, and pull the thread in.
- ☐ Cut out four body parts, place the two parts of the front on top of each other, and stitch a 0,5 cm seam at centre front (Sketch 13c, point 2). Repeat with the two other parts forming the back. Remember always to place the fabric right sides together. Press the two seams slightly.
- ☐ Stitch the side seams of the two arm parts (Sketch 13c, point 3).
- ☐ Fold a 0,5 cm casing along one raw edge, and gather this folded part with strong thread (Sketch 13b, point 4). The completed gathered edge should measure 1,6 cm. Place one felt hand between the two layers of fabric (Sketch 13b). Stitch the seam, and turn right side out. Repeat with the other arm. Fill lightly.
- ☐ Lay the front part of the body right side up. Place the raw edge of the arm between the two marked places (Sketch 13c, point 6). The part of the arm marked with a dotted line falls in the seam (Sketch 13c, point 7). Place the back over the other two parts, right side down. Stitch the seam (Sketch 13c, point 8).
- ☐ Stitch a continuous seam of 0,5 cm along the inner leg (Sketch 13c, point 9), and cut a notch between the legs (Sketch 13c, point 10).
- ☐ Fold a 0,5 cm casing over and gather the raw edge of the foot parts (as for the hands). The gathered part must measure 2,2 cm.
- ☐ Place the felt feet between the two layers of fabric, and stitch the seams (Sketch 13c, point 14).
- ☐ Turn the body part right side out, and fill lightly.
- ☐ Fold a 0,5 cm casing at the neck part (Sketch 13c, point 11) and gather this section with strong thread.
- ☐ Sew the head, with the gathered part at the back, onto the body.
- ☐ Make hair loops with yellow wool, and sew onto the head (see photo).
- ☐ Stitch the hat seam with right sides together. Turn right side out.
- ☐ Fold a 0,5 cm casing over (Sketch 13d, point 12), and place on the head so that the gathered part of the head is under the hat. Sew the hat on.
- ☐ Gather the nose (Sketch 13c) as for the head, fill tightly and sew along the dotted line (Sketch 13c, point 13).
- ☐ Cut eyes from the felt, and paste them on.
- ☐ Draw the eyebrows and mouth with marking pens.
- ☐ Colour the cheeks with blusher.
- ☐ If you wish, tie a narrow frill around the neck.

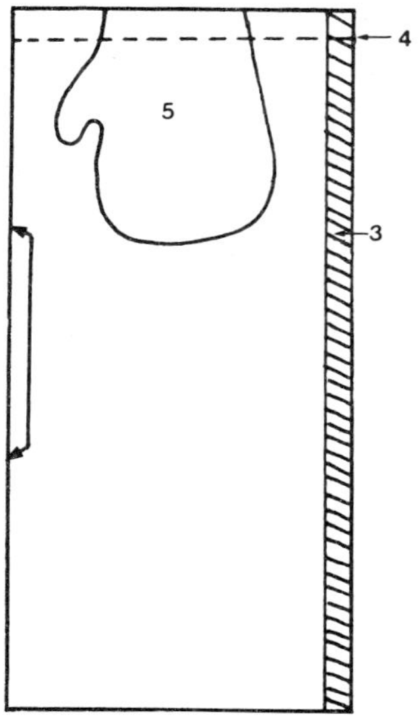

Sketch 13b

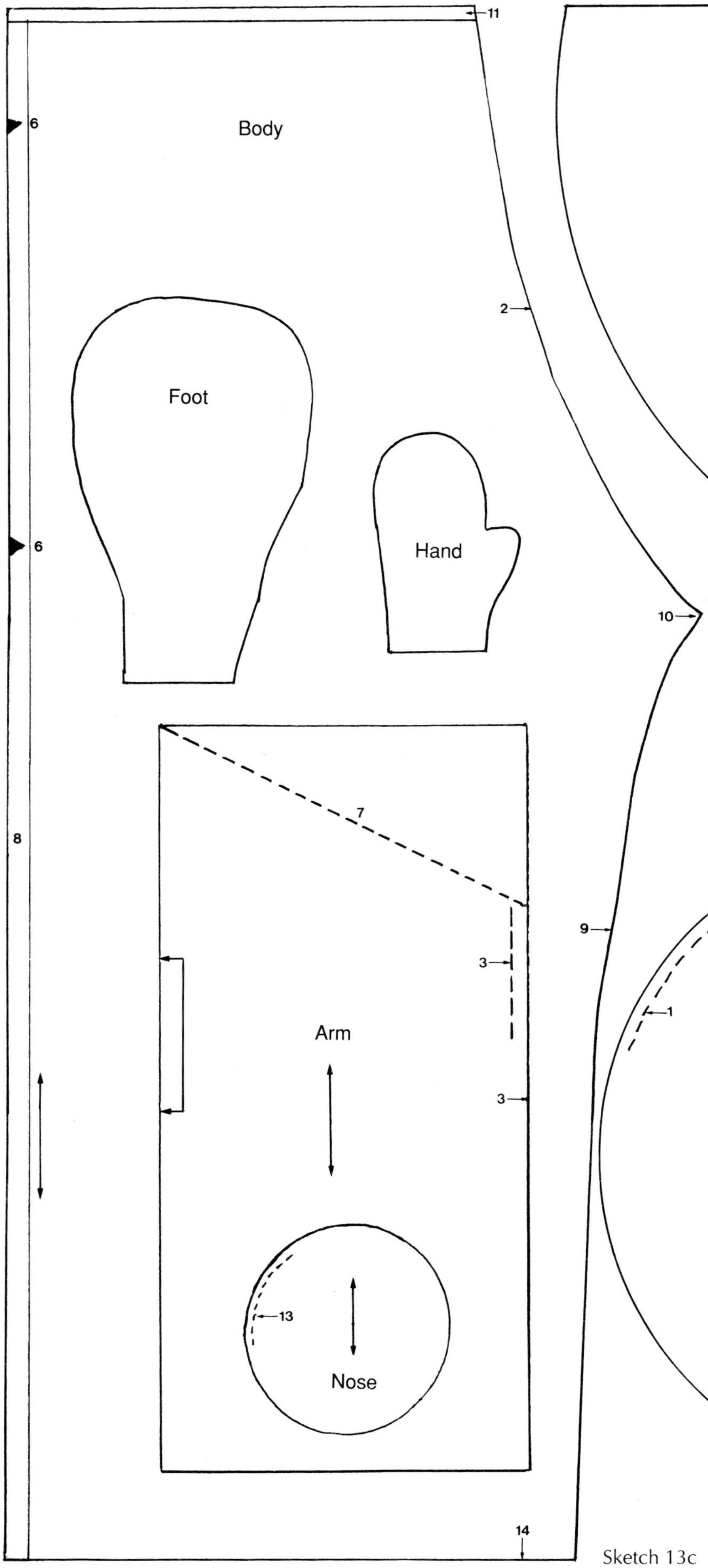

Sketch 13c

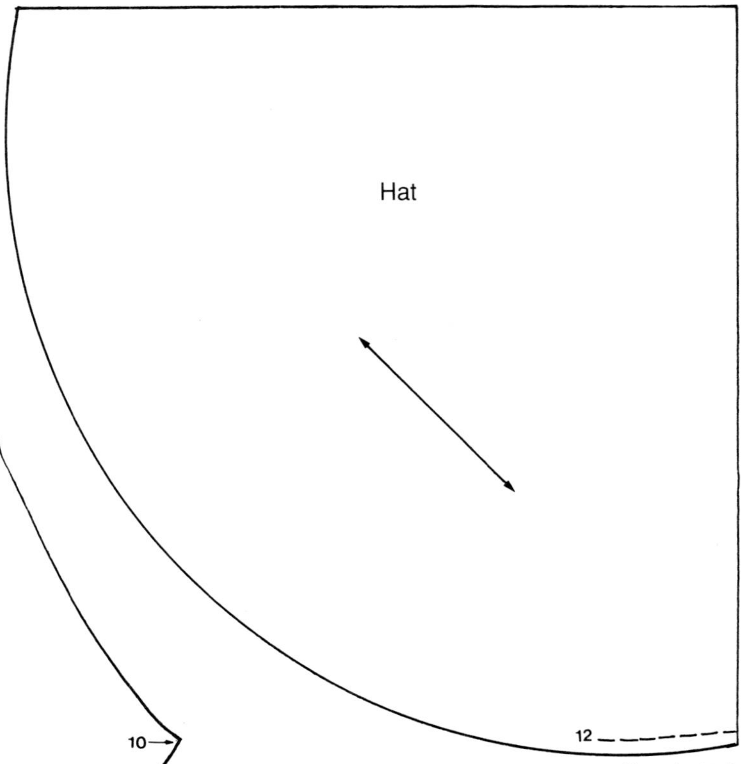

Sketch 13d

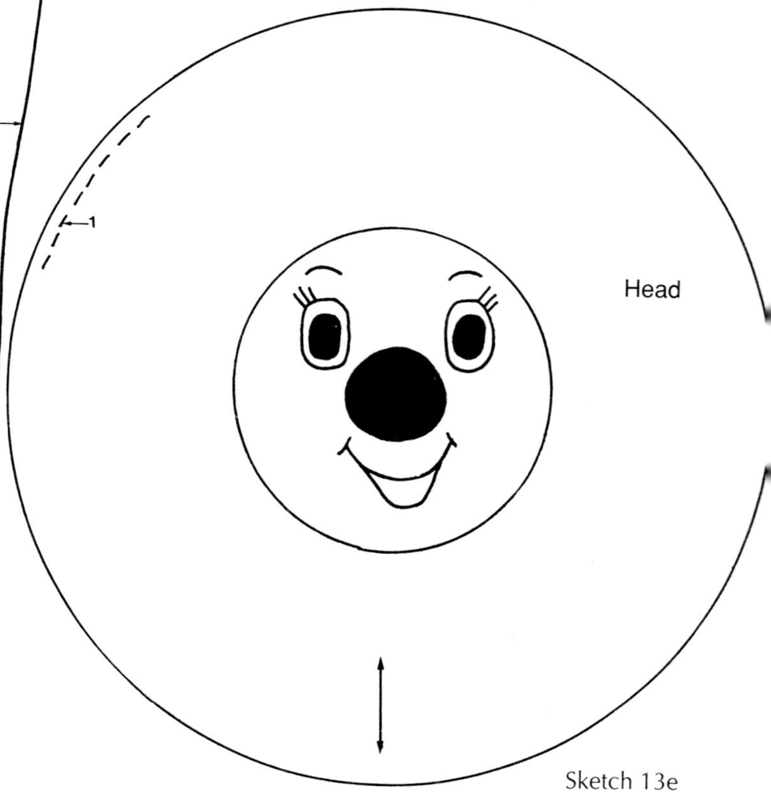

Sketch 13e